INSIDE MY MIND

BY

MUNDY MUNDY

© 2018 by Mundy Mundy. All rights reserved.
Published by Vantage Point Publishing
Indianapolis, IN 46205

No part of this publication may be reproduced or transmitted in any form or by any means, electronic or mechanical, including photocopy, or any information storage and retrieval system, without permission from the publisher. The only exception is a brief quotation in printed reviews.

Limit of Liability/Disclaimer of Warranty: While the publisher and author have used their best efforts in preparing this book, they make no representations or warranties with respect to the accuracy or completeness of the contents of this book and specifically disclaim any implied warranties of merchantability or facilities for a particular purpose. No warranty may be created or extended by any persons. The advice or strategies herein may not be suitable for your situation. You should consult with a professional where appropriate. Neither the publisher nor author should be liable for any loss of profit or any other incidental damages, including but not limited to special, consequential, or other damages.

This is a work of fiction. Names, characters, businesses, places, events and incidents are either the products of the author's imagination or used in a fictitious manner. Any resemblance to actual persons, living or dead, or actual events is purely coincidental.

ISBN **978-1-943159-11-6**

LCCN 2018908693

The publisher would appreciate notification where errors occur so that they may be corrected in subsequent printing and/or editions. Please send comments to the publisher by emailing to deeprivers67@yahoo.com

Printed in the United States of America

BIO

Mundy Mundy born in Indianapolis, Indiana is a versatile poet looking to bring something different to the minds of readers. Using word manipulation and deep thoughts to enhance the dreams of all who dare to dream.

DEDICATION

To my lovely children, my mother and father and of course my brothers. Let my footprints guide your path and Thank You for allowing me to dream.

SHUFFLING THE CARDS

Once upon a time in a land just around the corner. A man lived a lie and harvested lots of drama. His mind was obstructed by sex and by money in the words of Sanford "YOU BIG DUMMY!!" love he used to manipulate the hearts of women to penetrate, he watched as what they once were slowly started to disintegrate. Evil pure evil a walk amongst the flames, a devil; a demon. Their outlook is the same. Karma was just a sideshow Misery was his main, a life of love and peace to him just seemed so plain.

But, like most things do he eventually grew, scratches became scars it was all brand new. The agony, the hurt, the tears in his eyes, his own disgust for telling a lie. Thoughts beyond self, the needs of others replaced his motto fuck another. The darkness fading from his heart gave his soul a chance to shine, what he was and what he was to become were two separate lines.

Repentance and forgiveness for his sins he begs before he sleeps, then again when he wakes and sometimes before he eats. Smiles are genuine overlapping the smirks, greed subsides and joy is birthed. The change is inevitable though the journey is long, his debit must be paid he knew right from wrong.

One day he shall stand as a beacon for hope, but till then I will just continue to outgrow my ghost.

THE SOURCE OF FEAR

My soul passes through the letters like the veins in my heart, giving life and purpose to everything written by these hands. I put all of me into every sentence; word after word stripping down, exposing more of myself for others to critique. Some pay homage fore what lies beyond their windows is similar to the appearance of the layout they see through mine. It's as if we have been synchronized from birth, how easily they relate to me.

Others scrutinize my approach unable to disable their closed minds, too afraid to inspect the box from an uncharted angle. I rebuke their coward ways, continuing to investigate the world from the outside inward. I like different.. Appreciating the courage of the nerd... Their uniqueness is inspiring. I too gravitate towards the unknown in search of change... can't eat the same shit everyday..

So I have decided to put something new on your plates.

Let's call it the oddball way of thinking. LeBron James everyone won't like the decision, but can't deny the results. Snap back they will adjust because not everything is one size fits all.

Gratitude is appreciated but never expected because some still dread the aliens.

Finally got that grey ... been searching for many years.. Always wanted it just didn't nowhere to find it.. Shit just kept coming back Kodak.. Like spooky dark; really black... hell it was an eclipse. All that could be seen were the windows to my soul ... hadn't yet learned to smile... Drained of hope departed from belief. it was like Edgar was stand on my shoulder quoting his famous words into my existence. Seems I was approaching things the wrong way puttin my shoes on the wrong feet walking in circles. Spinning around and around 360 standing in the same place. No chance of change... No unfamiliar territory. Been here dun dun it.. Same ole same ole.. Then I find my way onto that two way street, staying away from the highways. It started to make sense, all that was needed... Q tips and some good reading glasses.

MORE THAN JUST A FEW LINES

Encrusted in the here and now.... living for the encore, built to last... Not for last; desire makes the dreams soar...

HER

Punished for my addiction to love, I have returned to your door with lust soaked linen father. Well you grant me access, I want to come home. Does the stench of our sweat deny me entry, is this the golden apple of paradise. It flows from her like nectar, the taste cause me to submerge into it. I thirst for it, I will uproot this world and give it to her. My desire knows no limit, Forgive me the warmth, sways my judgment, I stand as King but not as ruler.

THEY FORGOT ABOUT YOU

Left to live amongst the rats, accessible to the fears of the common man. Treated like a slave by your fellow man. Loyalty... what loyalty ... didn't even tell you they were moving? All the work you put in.... only to be marooned in ruins. Foolishly you strive to win the favor of those who owe you a favor. They split up all 40 acres even sold the mule and you got nothing... aint that some shit beyond being cruel. At times it seems like the pets are more endeared ... you cry and suffer... Your hatred is warranted just the focus is wrong. Your color schemes are disoriented, you're on the wrong team... they said fuck you; then fucked you. Now your Lucifer... Kane and Able... Bad Santa wants to destroy everything. Mad because the sky is blue ... it's a shame that your pain won't let you see... They forgot about you.

A CHANGE IN DIRECTION

Please don't scold the messenger; I was programmed to reject the originals. They have deemed too many unreachable, I was created to extend that reach. Maybe it's the products they use that causes all the streaks or maybe it's just a vision thing, seeing only what they choose to see. They prance around like heroes, now they're just shepherds without their sheep. The flock has had enough.. Rerouting... In this class we really teach, substance in the dialogue, methodically adjusting prior beliefs. What's offered here.. Was never there and never will it be.

RAIN RAIN GO AWAY

The rain pours falling rapidly downwards, splashing as it repeatedly hits the mark. The echoing tone of water diving into a puddle of itself, registers for what seems to be miles; in truth only a chins length away. The puddles ripple as the wind passes over, whistling in short quick breathes.

Raindrops get heavier as the storms become more aggressive, calming for brief moments then intensifying as dark clouds settle in. Bitter like ocean water unable to be consumed, salty residue tracks illuminate the direction of the rain. Then with a thud the tree crashes, no longer able to stand. Even its roots can't hold it upright for on this day the storms are too strong and nothing has meaning.

YOURS TRULY

Don't take my smile from me... Please don't remove my joy. I need to be here, my desire is to be loved... don't falsely remove the stars from my eyes. Nor the calm from my spirit.. For they are all that warms my heart. The icy bitterness of loneliness still chases me. Open the door let me in I don't want my heart to die.. It's all I have left to give you.. I will leave it here for you, please take care of it... for I could not. It deserves a better life, I want it to grow up knowing that it was meant to be... kind. It was meant to be ...felt. It was meant to be ...strong. It was meant to be yours.

HE WHOM LAUGHS LAST

Not quite the pinnacle... have a few miles left.. Before residing in my kingdom at last... tired of the Warriors life... rather pass than shoot... armor has a few rust spots... No need for oil... Bout to take it off... I have signed the letter... mounted my weapon... took a spot next to the Queen... my kingdom is my sanctuary. Some yell obscenities as if they have been betrayed, maybe next time you will extend that bet beyond the roulette wheel. My downfall was never in question because I have never asked. Instead I hobbled across the stripe, admired the scars and said thanks. Things could have been worse some didn't finish the race ...disqualified, eliminated or just didn't get the date. They always said the odds were stacked against the chosen few. They just never said who the oddballs were they were referring to ... on the job training... learn as you go.... A1 student.... passed the course. Uprooted myself climbing above the hatred. Their futile attempts to produce the rebirth of a now ancient warrior have fallen short. Masterfully I mastered the key positions in life... finding peace with just my piece. Now my facial expression is upside down.

TELL THAT BITCH I AINT HOME

If karma is the bitch... then who is this whore at my door calling her self depression? Peeking through my peek hole; staring at me staring at her. She is like that fat cock blocking friend denying me of a happy ending. I assume she wants company but I have no idea why it's me she chooses to aggravate. I wiggled through the crowd hoping that someone else would grab her attention... I just want to be alone. She dun been with way too many for me tah ever desire a romance with her. I have seen her work... a trail of broken hearts, slit wrist, head shots, and overdoses. Front page of an obituary; dark clouds over picnics; she can fuck up a wet dream.

Okay you got me I will keep it real I know the hoe we partied a little back in the day, nothing serious though. I was lonely, feeling kinda lost had the weight of the world on my shoulders and she caught me sit by myself doing nothing... we drank and danced to a few old slow songs. However, as our conversation flowed on I realized this freak was into somethings I just wasn't into. Jumping off of bridges, playing Russian roulette, hanging from a ceiling fan, it just wasn't my thang. I was working on my intro; she was all about the outro. I didn't see no common ground that's all. So I left didn't even kiss her I said goodbye.

Guess she took it like I dissed her, cause I started dance with her sister Hope, but shit she had a style that I liked. Now ever time Hope come through she want to come too... I just can't handle two women in my life. Plus, hope is expecting... our love child is coming soon ...and ain't no room for depression with Success in the House.

THOUGHTS IN MY HEAD

I dreamed I was dreaming the skies were grey and the rain was red. Humanity was sinking and the birds all fled. People in robes screamed off with their heads. The verdict was in ...OFF WITH THEIR HEADS... some paced the floor other just rest in bed going over their life ...thoughts in their head.

Then there were those who used an unbalanced chemical balance to progress throughout their day, networking through addiction sleeping their pain away ...sobriety brings truths no matter how much they induce can't escape... thoughts in their head.

In my dream I dreamt my sheets were walking they hated the way I smelled. Fearing my skin they wanted me dead. To them I was unfit to fit anywhere; I was a beast among beauties... thoughts in their head.

Before I awoke I prayed that it was just a dream and the world wasn't really like what I had seen. Only an illusion... a nightmare... bad dream... a mirage ...ugly fantasy. A thought in my head

I AM YOURS

Your eyes make me weak but your touch strengths me.... I am addicted to your beauty and in love with your voice.... Your smile comforts me ... Your lips inspire me... I cherish the moments when our bodies are one with each other... Make love to me with your heart ...wrap me in your essence ...feel my pulse quick I am aroused by you... for you ...I want you ...take my love and my soul will surrender... You are mine and I am yours.

HERE I AM

Give me my vengeance let those whom mocked me, wallow amongst the ruins of the shit storm I leave in my wake. Let them fear my success as they kneel before the headlines. My arrival was guaranteed, never questioned one yellow brick in the road. I knew I was on the right street.
Not yet polished though ....more like a semi-gloss, but, working my way up to diamond status. This is not a dream them shitz is like illusions, this right here... this is ground breakin, cracks in the concrete. Heavy; Jaw dropping, heart racing... alright now... you could say I'm on one! Taught to stand strong, the deeper the roots the firm the tree stands. I am trying to get my Brady on not the comeback cause I ain't going nowhere... I mean that champion level, where I can say kiss my ass... I made it.

IDENTITY CRISIS

Puppeteer no puppet... look ma' no strings. Yes that has a purpose... all things have a purpose or what's the purpose. Not Oscar worthy... how can this be... the best novel ever written and converted to the big screen. Every star has a role it's the greatest story ever told. Cut! Some of you have fallen out of character... forgotten your lines... standing on stage, when you should be hold the door. Hold the door... when it your turn to stand in the light... this movie has a budget and poor production can cost you your life. Can't afford too many takes to get your scene right. Our audience awaits... they grow impatient... can't keep making mistakes... to earn your spot on the walk of stars... you must perfect your character. Know who you are...

QUESTIONS NO ANSWERS

Theories on life unorthodox... Thinking before the box... Like why the cracks exist in the pillars of my window seat or how water keeps seeping in... Anger tempts me to return to where I was spawned and raise my sword... standing in front of my shield ...no barriers... transgressions formulate to tragedies as I tether towards the unforgiven. I've work so hard... God knows I've worked so very hard... turning my back on the unknowing... dining on a fine cuisine of information... didn't eat too fast, had to watch for bones... some shit just seems fishy... unfamiliar with that life; in my life experiences... Hell I didn't even know what posh meant... distracted by the view just outside my radius… Unhappiness makes its move. Undetermined... Wasted thoughts navigating towards that cardboard box ...Eddie Kane... solo career... better think this one through. Honestly I don't know how 2 speak on my feelings... I am use to doing things on my own... I have fallen off course of my original destination... struggling to get back on track... Everything that once use to ease me ...now only serves to irritate me... I have lost all joy, dwelling in limbo... Confused waiting on a sign or is it waiting on me?

RIGHT OUT IN FRONT

Dry blood has been chiseled from the nail bed of these hands. Fingerprints have forced their way onto the flesh of my biblical brothers and sisters. Lack of understanding once commanded my life, angry assisted... Gilligan... Lies camouflaged my true intent... mask on... King no Kingdom ...half ass prepared my soldiers now prayer is my hero. Comfortably resisting growth... Desire died with the dream. Money over bitches... me over everything… should have moved my loved ones to safety. Bridge buster... shook a lot of hands cut as many wrists. Flawed flawlessly past perfection... master's degree in screw up. Show up to show out... just never showed up. Loved to be loved but loved no love ...Selfish. Chance after chance just a slap on the hand. Wo is me demeanor no sign of fortitude. Dark wing duck... can't stay out of my own way most times. Had to exhale... Bitter bunny rabbit... won't obstruct the view... put it all on the table. Right Out In Front.

IN BETWEEN THE LINES

I was told I had a flow to my style... Rhythmatic structure to my thought pattern. I think it's the way I prepare each sentence, just sounds like music to your ears. I mean I stand at the fence with the world and relay that juicy gossip. Sometimes it can feel like morning coffee or hot sex and a cigarette. The truth when applied truthfully minus all the dirt. Has a chance to reach its target, I am proof it truly works. The trials that lead to my autonomy were brilliantly performed. Broken down and rebuilt; Broken down and rebuilt.. Repeatedly, until I was both humbled and grateful. What I share with you is more than what you see, these words I use to inspire you, lose power if you just read.

GLASS HOUSE

It's nothing that hasn't been done before, I am not the originator nor have I laid the blueprint. There are several that wear my scars and tell my story, many footprints clutter my path. My sins are shared by an abundance of groupies. Gender does not separate or distinguish ...Unisex... one hell fits all. The rules weren't written to shed light on me; they were too signed and dated before my time. Still the errors of my ways seem to be a ladder for others to step upon, but their own mischief contains them. While evading the stones they cast. I notice the walls begin to crack; the roof leaks and the floors crumble underneath their feet. They must have thought this was a two way mirror, but it's just glass and all can be seen. What's visible to one is visible to all. So your stones we don't need

MOST VALUABLE PEMMANSHIP (MVP)

Steph Curry with the lingo. It's good from anywhere. Sick shot always in range. Throwing rocks in the ocean...can't miss. Bred to do this shit, it's a blood thing. Premeditated I was given the gift, backed into a corner still clutch bitch, you could say I got an angle of this. Always knew I was good with words, dreamed of being a champion. Dedicated... I'm talking about practice. Had to put the work in... like to show out. When I show up. Addicted to the feel of metal on my hand.. My precious. Top of the food chain. Star power... Hard act to follow... the new window cleaner.

SACRIFICE OF SIN

Who are you to ask this of me? I dare you I have already given of myself. So doubtful are the masses, you ungrateful vultures. Waiting for the stench to invade your nostrils. Betrayal is your weapon of choice, what a fool you are, you make me laugh. Does my posture resemble that of easy prey? Why do you assume that my soul, shall just surrender. I am a replica of he who gave you purpose, I am the brother of the chosen one. I am the reason why Lucifer flies no more, the cause of sin and the breath of vengeance... know my name and fear my kind ... I am Man!!!

WORDS DISORDERED

The dialogue constructed to constrict doubt, prospers in supplying conversation that curves ignorance. Cerebral lubrication... Stimulating your emotions to respond. Digest the scripture let it cleanse your diaphragm.

Preliminary steps to violent illusions brought to life through an intellectual gift. Some deem it Wordplay... a masterfully cunning approach to deliver cover for those seeking shelter from the content of their true feelings....

Let's Get High! Razor sharp, shogun blade, intent to kill, dark blood, bone jarring war wounds. Words placed in aggressive order ...Gun play.

It's not the current that you see, but the one underneath that snatches the oxygen from your lungs. It was never the river; it's the things in the water that await the slaughter of the sheep, whom venture to close to the stream. So watch where you swim cause not all use their pens to celebrate these worldly perks. Some seek retribution through verbal execution… this ain't what you want. The cluttered mind of a word hoarder, an author with a word disorder.

WHERE IS THE GARDENER

Where did I put those brushes I must paint, the world needs color. Some seem so blank. Dissolving into indistinguishable configurations with complimentary personalities. They continue to seek out their fore father's pathway, as if they are unaware of their failures...generational insanity...this gets complicated... Legions of liars compromise the direction of the sunlight, needed in order for the flowers to blossom to their full potential. Thus causing the flowers to behave more like weeds, spreading their ugly throughout the fields... self-made inhibitors. Justifying their shameful acts, by channeling historical events. They rapidly drain the nutrients from the very lands that feed them, WHERE IS THE GARDENER? Tell him the resources are minimal and the flowers struggle to maintain their soul. Tell him the fight remains in their heart but, their hands are tied. Tell him his chemicals only make it harder, for them to see beyond the here and now..... No better yet tell him ...we have decided to rid the yard of weeds our damn self...

THE PAN HANDLER'S STORY

Shit dun got deep she says I got to go ... she don't want me no mo... Where is Mr. Clark when ya need him? Simple politics my minuses are adding up and my pluses are subtracting... never was good at math. I did watch the electric company so I know when something... don't go there... my hearts been broken I 'm on some bipolar shit. I got it firsthand the love is still there, walked right by the farmer spoke directly to the horse. This aint about love ...it's the principals... been spending a lot of time in the office. Intentions A+ got to see the heart was in the right place, it was biology were the issues occurred... priorities all messed up.. Woodbine... can't get right. Get rich schemes dreaming during working hours... Dreams far-fetched need to drum it down a bit. Warm milk at night time ...calm down, damage done scars tighten the skin... can't fool her with the okie doke... nope seen too much... knows how it's supposed to look, love is blind... It's A Miracle She Can See!!!!! The fool in this story is me foolishly playing this hand should have shuffled the cards... wrote a poem about it ... smooth talker dun hit a few bumps rocky road, my house is not my home .. Luther dead.

THANKS FOR COMING

What has been done to remove me from your eye? I was that twinkle; now I am a fallen eyelash, removed for constricting you from seeing beyond me. Though it appears you continuously look through me. Even as I take my walk of shame... head down, back hunched, tears refusing to cease. I notice the pain in your posture. I can hear the sorrow in your speech... this is our encore.

NOW 4 LATER

May I have your attention please....I would like everyone to direct your eyes towards the front as the mission is ahead of us. Our future is riddled with hopelessness. The desire to be more has made many less. The worthy are destined to be worthless. Leaders regress to followers.... men to boys ....women to whores... we must combat these issue with prejudice for nothing ever have we faced with such a commitment to destroy. How long will we monitor these acts genocide before we move forward? For some the very thought of curing this situation cause great grief. Fore to address your brother and sister, with malice in the heart ....words are useless. However the need to ensure a richer future takes precedence over all. What must be done; shall be done or man will surely extinguish us. Fall victim not to the falsehood of love; instead open your mind to a more realistic acknowledgment of your worth. Understanding that the blood was spilled, so that we may redeem ourselves. Live to open doors; for the ones who inspect the trails, as they walk the path behind us. Give of yourself now for later.

FREE AT LAST

Diluting my thoughts drowning them in fantasies, looping visual compensation. Cravings for understanding, knowledge in abundance my mind gets the bubble guts. No chaperon for penmanship, the words have free range. Prisoners of their shell no longer, nor slaves to human emotions. Free at last this vibrant glossary of verbal seduction is free at last. Executed by the tongue of a free thinking dictator. Spread upon the masses like falling rain, illustrated in the conduct of his followers, his visions comfort their pain. Words become like portals, opening universal doors to worlds unknown. The ignorant stand in the doorway, while the unbridled witnesses move onward.

BURNING THE WINGS OF AN ANGEL

Challenge neither its courage nor its intent for the wise know that evil bears many fruit. It comes for us all, our presence has been requested. Our souls have been marked we must atone. No longer will our brother take the forefront for the sins of man. No longer shall our father be merciful. The windows slam shut, as the hourglass quickly removes time from our existence. The sandman is coming and Grimm draws the curtains closed. Sins thought to be removed will be replaced, the rich shall drown and the poor shall rise. The halls of hell will fill with the smell of burning feathers, for on this day the fallen will never fly again.

FORGETFUL MINDS

You said you wouldn't hurt me ... what happened to that...
you said I was important to you what happened to that...
you said it was me and you what happened to that.. I gave
you my hurt you said I had nothing to fear...what happened
to that?

LOST

Warm burst of sunshine press against the skin. Taking my soul to a blissful woosah.., challenging me to dance to a new beat. Melodies course through my veins, the rhythm coats my flesh. My heart pounds like the snares in a drum line, thoughts of you complete the symphony. An arrangement so emotional and persuasive, that my body no longer belongs to me.

MISSING U

My heartbeat quickens, my breath shortens.... I feel as if the world spins no longer, as even time has decided to stand still. Pain courses through my body and my soul cries out. Misery, torment, crushing, gnawing, and ripping. The agony forces my mind to wander. Darkness, shadows and gloom engulf me. Showering over like tidal waves they smash across the memories and wash them from my view. I stand, wait, dream, and remember we are to be....

I miss you

THE FINAL EXAM

Lost is my beginning drowning in my past; preexisting solutions to a nightmarish reality, sprinkled along the pathway. How foolish it must have seemed tarnishing a legacy for moments. Submerging my innocence into the fire only to see if it burns. Then helplessly observing my soul melting away right before my eyes. Stupidity congratulates the efforts to consume the in-consumable, it relishes in the small print. Fixated on a truce that each footprint has meaning, that each soul has purpose. I re-emerge bloody and battered but, stronger than ever.

MOTH WITHOUT A FLAME

Brutally honest peers see not the pain they cause. Their speech hinders hearts from loving and awakens the beast. Dabbling in dialogue containing poison in its contents. They ravage the spirits of their prey. Leaving them shamed and deflated... Empty.

Agonized by the constant torment.

Unjustly punished for their singularity, shunned for their gifts, hated for amusement, ridiculed for their appearance. These hollowed victims walk amongst us; hearts blackened, corroded, bitter, cold, ugly and undefined, wandering in search of their moment... Seeking only their flame.

INCEPTION OF A MAN

Hidden inside the words my story flows freely. I have benefited from the tears that dampen their eyes. I have taken gratitude in the pain caused when my name is uttered through trembling lips. Now I have sheathed my sword, the smell of blood no longer arouses me. No longer do I crave the darkness, the path I walk glows, I have been redirected.

The proclaimed eater of worlds is full, I can't take another bite. I come in peace, wishing you no harm.

Laughter conceals doubt but the eyes unveil truths... they glare at their oppressor, witnesses to my shortcomings. Victims of my sword of chaos.

Bearers of rage and retribution... strike if you will.

Humbled though not healed, recovery time runs concurrent with life span. The source of fear lays within, dismantling my truths adding more windows for me to see through. I share not in my souls amusement, never liked Roller coasters. Though unknowingly it appears I have lived my whole life on the tracks.

This is where I get off; the first tiger with vertical stripes. I am learning a new trick or two. His plan is my plan, formulated before me, for me. The trials begin

THE THORN IN MY BED

Violently sculpting an ensemble of moments, with bizarre realities. Phasing in and out of tranquility, submitting to irrelevant thoughts, as they run a muck. Past, present and future mix like gumbo, twisting desires, wants and needs. Fabricating truths and lies; pain so much pain. Silent screams, abandoned by oxygen, a Dead-man's float, drowning. Visions end as they begun, spinning vigorously, turn on the lights, so I can see this monster. His approach it stealth, he moves when I least expect it, when my will to fight is at its weakest point... destroying my dreams like a thorn in my bed.

HEARTLESS

A fig tree that bears no fruit... An ocean with no water... The sky with no stars... Walls without floors. Abused, abandoned, mistreated. Lonely, exiled, diminished. Wizen from love, it becomes dark like coal and twice as hard. Tamper proof; protected from further mortification. Reluctant to receive, with nothing to give. Love struck, rendering scars and sorrow. Numb, refusing to let emotions reside. Once so beautiful... Alive... full of passion, now damaged, cold, heartless.

PARADISE

Take my hand and enter my world, stroll with me across my lands. Listen as the birds sing to us; witness the fragrances the flowers shed. Remove your shoes so that you can feel the land beneath your feet. Relax as the air swirls through your hair. Notice how softly it's caress your being, what a wonderful scenery we have before us. Now open your eyes and cherish these moments for after this you will know...

APOLLYON'S PLEA

Undo this wretched curse; fore I don't want to love. I have no desire to care for others. Disarm my heart, allow the darkness to harden. My only passion is for their demise to rip souls from their habitat. Don't leave me bonded to your commandments, allow me to roam free. Take not my hatred, instead rid me of happiness. Watch me manifest and evolve, like a cancer gnawing at the very seams of survival.

Let all who come before me, be riddled with the same destiny, to dwell forever more in my sanctuary of insanity.

THE RETURN

I glance at us through the eyes of the unseen. I stand witness as our galaxies gather and our world's embrace; planets circle one another dancing amongst the stars. Enriched hues fill the sky, harmonious sounds collide with each breath, a flirtatious noise tempting my inner self to remain focused on cosmic illusions which push reality out of existence.

BRAIN FREEZE

What if we have not been forgiven? What if that's all a lie? What if heaven on earth is but, an obscene gesture that only serves to comfort you? What if we have all been punished and Earth is a term meaning "Hell"? Would you be shocked to know that Lucifer was not the only angel banished? I mean look at mankind and all that it has brought upon any and everything it comes in contact with. Man is a destroyer....there is nothing holy about any of us. I mean okay I will give you newborns and babies, they are innocent of wrongs. However, once they have been exposed to this world, their innocence is no more. Then there are the ones who believe that they are forgiven for damn near anything as long as they pray for forgiveness. There are some passages that clearly contradict that theory. I mean seriously what if we are from different worlds but, all banished here until our life force leaves us? That would explain a lot of things about our differences. It could also give reason to why we worship differently and even to why images of Gods look objective to each other. Who knows maybe we are just as we have been told...but, what if we are not?

A MOTHER'S LOVE

She trembles in fear knowing that her days are not as tall as they use to be. I stand in the window, watching as she continuously cries out. Her tears roll through the fields and over the trees. Screams bellow, stars flicker, and the skies strike back. The ones who know the truth; those who have always remained as they were to be in the beginning. Frantically race away as if they sense her grief becoming more powerful than she. Horrified glancing over the pages chapter after chapter ripped from the spine. She reminds her Judas of their betrayal, her voice whisk away dreams like a broom to an ant hill. Her tantrum provokes the mountains to bleed and the brightest star to hide. But, vengeance is not her message, fore a mother does not seek reprisal from her children. She is merely offering a clearer view of what shall pass, if we don't listen.

LEGACY

I have ran from my feelings and hid from my heart. The stares of a demon have broken me, I now drench myself in sorrow. It has been so long since I let him speak but, his tongue can no longer be contained. He beckons for flesh and desires to kill. I am his puppet and he plucks my strings, burning in the flames I see no way to break his spell. Then again I truly don't desire to, I am the bringer of darkness, the destruction of light. I am the new face of fear, the legacy bearer of Grimm.

RUNAWAY

Let no light shine consume the skies in darkness for eternity. Remove the stars from above, dim the moonlight, and eclipse the sun. Take the glimmer from the eye and the glow from the Aurora. Hide Hide... I tell you, run and hide. Let it be known judgment is coming and we have all been looking out the wrong window.

STANDING BEHIND A ROCK

Entrapped… wisdom has abandoned me.. I see no light... my tongue has been removed.. no light. The thoughts... the words… I have been robbed... I have been condemned to silence. I must touch them they need me. I am trying to process this with no evidence or reason... someone has taken from me. Gone all gone… my pain... My laughter... my love... my story...replaced by nothing… blank space... a universe of blank space. No antidote. What is the cure... no light... please come back ... no light... I have nothing without you... no light... wait... It has returned to me, I am restored back to my love... I return. I remember now every thought so clear ...my voice has risen.. I am whole once more. Let me begin I have so much fire inside of me.. my passion no thought ... no voice ...no light..

A GAME OF TAG

It was the chatter that shielded the slap. The music cloaked the echoes of pain, Mercy had no place here, it was nowhere to be found. Sharp were his horns but that smile, cheek to cheek… nose to chin. Reminded me of that episode when Joker bested Harley Quinn. The pitter patter of tiny souls, frantically racing chasing after her, safety is just a illusion, shit he just tired right now, then the headlights flash. He cheatin fo' real now. Approaching like a pimp slow ridin next to the curb, speaking a bunch of nonsense, at least that's what we heard. Pawns never know what the royals are saying; they only know sacrifice can become real at any time. She must be through running or crazy, maybe she is still woozy that ass whoopin was a doozie. Look at this lamb walking gingerly to the slaughter. The music goes up, and the tears revisited my view. Then the souls bellow out as they always do....

INSIDE MY CLOSET

I know u would ...stand next to me, walk, run, giggle and smile for me. I foresee you close to me, holding me, kissing me, telling me you loved me. I heard you laugh with joy in your heart and speak with passion in your voice. I heard, seen and felt it all...

I know I love you, I feel it in my chest when I think of you. I know I care because I want 2 protect you. I know it's real I can feel it; I want to spend my life with you.

All these things I have said when I am next to you ...I have taken it all for grant, realizing now I have yet to show you, that not only do I love you I live for you?

THY WILL BE DONE 6:10

Forbidden truths arranged to conquer suggested fables in sequence. Thinning the herd, re-configuring what was... what can be... and what is tolerable. Let us relapse ...anxious to establish existence, mortals masquerade as immortals. Undermining those believed to be mindless. But unspoken doesn't mean unknown, nor does it project intelligence. Ignorance sheds as information is divulged; peeling back the layers, rapidly gaining ground. Imbecility stuns momentum but progression is Ali in the 8th... Dope! Thy will be done... as challenges by trendsetters to continue to dream, inspire the creation of a new day.

ENDLESS

Floating through the universe, dancing on the galaxy floor. Lost in a parallel universe adjacent from the stars. Somewhere between now and forever drifting towards the sun. Silenced only by the whispers of an angel, a broken heart seeks to be loved.....

AM I STILL UGLY

Paralyzed in a thought pattern, I begin to stain the walls of my mind with an onslaught of voyages. Deep inside the regions of my inner-self, I have tried to prepare a world of happiness. The fact that I cannot truly find that happiness in which I seek, at times seems to destroy my mental safety.

Do I dare ask for help? Exposing what I feel to be my world of paradise. Uninhabited by the parasites that have infested my life for so long, the fools whom try to endanger everything that shines in my window of hope. What is it that they want or desire? Have they chosen to erase me? And if so, why must it be such a slow, brutally emotional death? I would prefer one behind the ear; maybe they know my deepest secrets. Maybe they understand that I choose to be free of the misery that the sunrise brings each and every day. Can that be? Can they actually hear what I think? God has watched me mistreat the angels of heaven; he has seen me embrace the said evil of this world. I have drank the blood of the innocent, time and time again. I still thirst! Yet, I feel it too! Just as he must, the beckoning of my soul to restore the joy I have swept out of so many lives. Could that be my calling? To repair the broken hearts. That would truly be a test, would it not? To try and regain a trust that I, myself have crushed. Though who I am truly trying to repair is me. I myself have fallen apart, engulfed by my own ignorance and self-pity. And with each passing day I add more and more fuel to the already burning inferno. Life itself has repeatedly smacked me in the face, I am told it is due to the wrongs but how can that be? Who has passed judgment on me? It cannot be God for he said on the Day of Judgment...Didn't he or have I been tricked again? I took all the mirrors down in my house, cause I am scared to see the real me. Yes, the Lord has made us all beautiful people but, sometimes the things we do to enhance our beauty only truly makes us ugly.

I wonder if I am still.....Ugly?

BURIED WITHOUT A TOMBSTONE

Peeking over the shoulder... observing from a distance... can't see shit! Too many obstacles in the way... Oblivious to the conversation... need to clean my ears... thought I heard my name... it was only the wind... Seems like their watching me... dying on the inside drowning in my tears... Wishing I was free chained to my past... Illusionist happiness disguises the hurt. Premeditated my torment was preconceived. Written before my arrival and finished before my passing. Just another toy in the toy box, forgotten in the waves of new ideas. Then discarded as if the world has Alzheimer, unable to recall the jubilation I supplied to their then so miserable lives. Used like an appetizer; when clearly I am the entrée. But, the impulse to dabble with confection encourages many to hurry through the gateway.

INSIDE MY MIND

I was just wondering if I should care that someone who looks like me is hungry? Should I care if their children have proper clothes to wear to school? Like should I give a fucc; that someone couldn't make it to work... even when I know they have no other means to take care of their family? Should I care that I see drug dealers hanging out in the same places children go to school and play? Is it any of my business that children are dying on my generations watch? Am I supposed to feel anything for young men and women who live in violence infested neighborhoods? When I see my people dying... when should I be part of the solution and when should I just mind my business? I mean as long as it's not me and mine ...Right!? I just wonder how do you know when your brother is your brother and when he is not? I mean I know Obama is one of ours... Shit he was president... can't deny him. Will Smith; Denzel, Beyoncé, Oprah, Maya, Steve Harvey. But, what about ol' girl from out west or dude from out East? Cuz from up North, damn near could be Bae from out South brother. I am just wondering when it's really cool to love your people. All Your People!!

INVISIBILITY

I have fallen like the angel of darkness, banished from paradise for my mistakes. Sentenced to live in a world that can't see me, alone, frightened, unloved and empty. In the shadows I reside far from human compassion, untouched, unknown, unforgiven and stripped of my sanity. Is this my beginning or shall it be my end. Must I grovel, lower to my knees or will my tears be your reward.

A DEMON'S RITUAL

Rage has reentered the fold. I don't know if it can be controlled anymore, temper mental off center. Lost my way back to the grey area, fumigating ... hot above the collar... steam passing through the pores. Fuck postal... shit going 4.20.99 ... Fred Krueger up all night just can't sleep.... shoulda let me be... now just want to Smash!! It's looking Grimm... Clobberin Time!! Momma raised a man... Daddy made me a fool... The streets bred a killer.. Humanity unleashed the Eater of Worlds. Light taker... nostrils flaring... eye squinting... heart racing ...fist clinched.. Can't take no more. Wayne... it feels like I am dying... not the physical form... the psychological is dissipating fast... remorse and mercy no longer have meaning ... immune to the pain of life evaporating... the stench has no effect.. No possession necessary.. Walked freely into the darkness... tired of the assumptions... Give 'em what they ask for... blood on my hands, flesh in my teeth it has begun... THE DEMON'S RITUAL

UNWRITTEN

Now I understand it was never meant to be understood.
Bunch of useless words no feeling... no substance...
Lifeless.

MUDSLIDE

Another hollow day, life is pushing me over the edge. Tried to make it to the top again... Jack and Jill. Not yet come to terms with my abilities, too eager to disagree. I know there is more to me, than what I have set free. Always told that a light shines upon me, still I have traveled in the darkness most of my days. Wanderer moved from life to life, just can't sit the fuck still. Continuously in the progress. No Progression... Fortunately no three strike rule in life... blessing and a curse. Repeat offender can't keep count. Misguided tour. Headed in the wrong direction, one too many do-overs, MJ moonwalk... sliding backwards. Adjusting to make necessary adjustments. Put extra tools in my toolbox, ready for work. Mike J for the rings... Mayweather in the ring... learn to win where others seem to lose... champion of champions' top of the food chain. Living witness of the MUDSLIDE.

DOOMED

Seductively serenaded by the illusion of immortality, Drained of spirit and faith, hopelessly we wander aimlessly without focus. Freed from responsibility and cursed by time. Devoured by demons the dream fades, while the nightmare of reality continues to feed. Mortality mercilessly demands compensation, and at that moment we are rendered choice less...

MY EYES

You ask for my desires, can you see my eyes? Your soul breathes new life into mine. Do I love you; cannot you feel my heart pound in my chest? Do my lips mean what they say, can you see my eyes? How can this be real, stare at the stars do they sparkle? Joyous are the angels whom watch over me, fore now they can rest their wings. No longer do they have to fear to leave my side. I am fulfilled, I have been made whole, my dreams are reality. Pain and sorrow chase me no longer. The angels can see my eyes. We, you and I, together, us what does it all mean, can you see my eyes?

QUIT FUCKING WITH MY HEAD

How can I overcome myself... it's not as easy as it may seem. My pedigree is survivor and my refusal to die... strangles my ambition to change... so I tussle... I will never just bend or break under pressure. I need to change to maintain. I will be more powerful than ever when this manifestation is complete... be you for that's all you can be...but, you can be so much more. I am following my dreams... if I just switch a few lines maybe I will get a shot. They love me... they love me not. Stand up and be heard shhh you talking to loud. You got to do you... don't forget about us. You must be dreaming... never stop dreaming. It all seems like bottle water and duct tape to me...

UNDEFEATED

I am just feeling like life is shorting fast. I am wondering how long I may have ...cigarettes, stress, high blood pressure, asthma and just the bumps and bruises of everyday living. Getting scared for myself I have escaped a lot of things in my time here but, no one escapes death it wins every time. We can only hope to delay it but, we cannot defeat it ....everyone loses to death it's the one thing that we as humans all share... it's the one thing that doesn't care about race, size, age or religion... When its deaths turn he always has the winning hand. So depressing just have a lot on my mind.... I guess.

THE DEVIL'S TEAR

Quench your thirst swallow every drop; let the essence of humanity fill your belly. O how good it must taste, sweetened by ignorance and flavored by our failure. Is this what you foreseen, when our father granted us life. A legion of fallen angels, plaguing the world. Were your cries of jealousy or were they merely a warning of what was to come upon our arrival.

IN THE HANDS OF THE AUTHOR

Change every paragraph, correct the sentences... check the spelling. Sharpen your pencils, bring a pen, do as you must. Erase that word and add another, don't say that name, be a hero. Do whatever you will but remain true to yourself and edit where necessary for your story is your own.

GRAVE DIGGER

Knew it was bullshit from the beginning stalled the inevitable just see if I could. Like to rattle the cage every now and then ...adds a little spice to the gumbo. Might just be a shit start ...let's see if I have gotten any better. Some of you have a heroin addict's resistance to your own fairytale. Your whole life has been Once Upon a Time. Character flaw after character flaw keeps you unrated... Eurhythmics.... All Saints... Honest. The laughter is not synchronized. You have been blacked faced. Justly ridiculed for your disobedient behavior... your feces infected conversation is visible even to the untrained eye...Glasshouse... hard to tell where you stand, can't keep it solid... tye dye cerebrum. No more soft shoeing... tough love... we know the truth. You're a structure of lies... a desert mirage... I was manifested to extinguish you... An alphabet master ...quick witted professor.. The Hoarder of Words returns. From window cleaner to grave digger... muthafucka watch yo tone..!!

A SINGLE MAN'S PRAYER

Awaken my heart, feed my soul, dance with me in the light.
Guide me towards the path of happiness and I shall not
impede the journey.

BLACK LIVES MATTER

Weak nigga, Bitch nigga, Fuck nigga, Broke nigga, Stupid nigga, Pussy nigga, Soft Ass nigga

Black Lives Matter

Trick bitch, Black bitch, Hood Rat, Tired ho, Slut, THot, Turnouts, Fake bitch, Nothing Ass bitch

Black Lives Matter

Single mother, Deadbeat dad, Broken home, Robbery, Rape, Murder, Domestic abuse, Senseless violence, Fuck that nigga

Black Lives Matter

Bloods, Crips, GD, VL, Drug dealer, Dropout, Mac10, 9 Millie, 45, 50 Cal, AK

Black Lives Matter.... But 2 whom?

PRAY 4 ME

Pray for me ...I am a sinner, my heart was full but my stomach was empty.

Pray for me ...my love was pure, anger became my thinner.

Pray for me ...fore I accepted the challenge, grew tired of the competition.

Pray for me ...I didn't know how high I had flown till I fell.

Pray for me ...I wanted to be normal, couldn't figure out what normal was.

Pray for me ...slowed my pace, the world sped up

Pray for me ...I can hear the music, but I refuse to dance.

Pray for me

THE SINFUL; SINLESS

Blame it on the angel of light; let his name be the reason for it all. Forget that we have choice; allow the persecuted to be judged by the sinners. Uproot their mustard seeds, filling the holes with doubt and shame. Shatter their hope and watch their strength decay. History has repeatedly spoken of our plot, the conquest has been well documented, but no blame do we bear. We are the Sinful Sinless and our shame is not our own.

FACE TIME

Personally doubt the personality can be enhanced enough to sustain anymore stains. Whole bunch of extra work mandatory overtime, got to get it done. The process to further the progression is a venomous one that only few dare to seek out. The same treacherous terrain; that once they called home. Now brings grief and sorrow to the thinnest fiber of their being. Incapable of vanquishing the rear view they instead become fixated on out running or hiding from it. But the lights of truth return the monsters to life and the distance between what was and what is becomes slim once again. Confrontation is the only remedy, for the liberation sought to surmount issues of our past, we must have moments with one's self.

LOVE

Trembling voices utter sounds unheard, foreseen by the watchers of this universe. Rewritten by its authors, spoken in unison by strangers from foreign lands. Its story has been spread, enhanced yet watered down. Ripped from the lips of Aphrodite, gliding on the wings of Cupid. Feared by the fallen, rejoiced by the innocent. Controlled by none and desired by all. Its name is as known as any before or after it, though it's origin in unknown. Pure energy conjurer of smiles and frowns as well as the prequel of life and death at times. Shallow a name used to describe those who deny it, sick are the ones who fall victim to it.

THE MASTERPIECE

Blank canvases prepare to attend a world of vibrant colors. Life changing hues, bold letters, bright lights and small print. Each canvas splashed with paint from an array of artist each leaving a piece of his or her self. Digesting and storing they feed and feed, becoming more and more alive. With each stroke they lose their purity, unknowingly giving away their innocence.

LOVED

Longing for the moment when I smile again. Praying for a solution to my tears, I search endlessly like the ancient hunters of the past. Where is my unicorn, my white whale, does not love exist. Show yourself to me; give reason to believe in you. Life has given me an empty bowl and I starve for fulfillment. An unfinished masterpiece submitted by a pain stricken artist. Why must misery continue to expose itself, I have seen and heard enough from it. Give what is needed to revive this hollow heart, fill it with potions of joy and comfort it..... Give it all to me and I will return it to you loved.

ENDLESS

Loathing through the universe, dancing on the galaxy floor. Lost in a parallel universe adjacent from the stars. Somewhere between now and forever drifting towards the sun. Silenced only by the whispers of an angel, a broken heart seeks to be loved...

THE APPLE

Soft passionate her kisses accept my flaws, her eyes enchant my being. Touching me seductively, her voice invades my mind. Let me lick you, my fingers caress, her silhouette. Surrender to me, gentle hands caress my face. I Inhale the scent, my lips her lips, her neck. Deep inside, her aurora embodies me, like a subtle wind. I want her. I want her not, I need her beside me ...in front of me, underneath me. I live to love her, die to protect her. My Queen, my Angel, my Apple.

SYBIL

Gestures of kindness have warmed my blood; I learned how to smile again. But contradictory thoughts continue to plague the here and now. Like a punchline that turns smiles upside down.

A QUICK SURVEY OF THE MENU

Presumed to have an intellectual deficiency. Aint always going to get the words right... However, my defiance of a courtship with the norm. Disables me from a thoughtless career as a yes man. Refusing to digest bad food just to amuse someone's need to communicate. Shit... I would rather starve than dumpster dive with a fool.

THE OTHER SIDE OF THE PILLOW

A bird flew to my house 2day ...we spoke about life, he had much to say. He told me how he had lost a friend to the black shadows in the water again and how his son was born with one wing shorter than the other. His wife left home to retrieve some food, when she was attacked by some monsters right next to the school.

He said he had no time to grieve because, the children were hungry they still had to eat. His findings were small but he couldn't travel too far, with the mother now gone and that alley cat in the yard.

He said he is hoping for rain because it might change some things, and he definitely needed some things to change.

Both his mother and father had passed, he couldn't remember when he seen his siblings last. Most of his friends went south for the winter; with everything going on he couldn't leave till December.

I listened and nodded as he explained his situation. By time he was done I just stood in amazement, then I went to my knees and said Thank You God for my vacation.

THE DEATH OF AN ANGEL

Where am I, these lands look familiar. I recognize the trails, though the roads wind different than before. Bumpier ...a few extra cracks. My shadow dies quicker now. I can't remember my dreams. The constant laughter... Dilutes my self-esteem... Hades has laid his eyes upon me before and I have rebuked his gaze. This seems different though, for it seems as if he has embodied my being. Sweat pours from brow. My tongue scrapes the roof of my mouth. Flames surround me but I don't burn. His horns protrude from my skull. His anger refurbishes my own. We stand in harmony like two lovers dancing under the stars. I can smell the evil as I am imprisoned inside sighed wings. Ankles bound by his slithering tail. We descend and then reemerge he speaks into my dreams, I am released... Sharp pain pierces my spine warm blood soaks my clothing. I stare as the forks of Hades rips through my chest hollowing my body. My loyalty has been betrayed.

NOT GOOD ENOUGH

I have changed the way I view the world, placing myself in the now.

Yet still I suffer.

My words are formatted with thought, softened by calm.

Yet still I suffer.

Dislike instead of hate, words instead of violence, love instead of loyalty.

Yet still I suffer.

My conscience is like a condom prohibiting me from making a mess.

Yet still I suffer

I stand naked exposing my true identity, holding back the stupidity that taught me to lash out.

Yet still I suffer.

Forward instead of backwards, hope instead of doubt, life instead of death.

Yet still I suffer.

Giver I have become no longer selfish, learned to extend my arms again.

Yet still I suffer.

Growing beyond where I had grew and still it's NOT GOOD ENOUGH.

SHATTERPROOF

Trying to behave but I keep losing the battle in my mind. Norman Bates.

They want us all 3-25-1971, Bangladesh. Lead by a horned leader 11-18-1978, with an invalid thought process.

Should have never turned my back on a coward 4-3-1882, lesson learned.

Nothing is forever, change is coming 1-20-2009. Can't believe anything I hear anymore 8-24-2006.

Seems like my peers would rather watch me fall than unsheathe their swords 3-14-1995.

Never needed the help anyway 1-17-1706, Atari 11-12-1980 man in a maze.

Vindictive 5-28-1357 got to get some shit off my chest.

Nothing like the usual, I swear it's in the water 8-14-2014. Gave a lot of myself to get to this point, but here I stand undefeated 1-14-1973 unduplicated, unbroken... shatterproof!

MEA CULPA

Black sheep shoulda left well enough alone. Always taking the extra step, removing the pillars, bridges unstable, demolition man.

Drama like hot sauce put that shit on everything.

No pain No gain made sure my loved ones lived plentiful.

Got a knack for dismissing the joy, party pooper professional.

Orphaned mannerism, unruly, rule breaker, loves the taste of golden apples. Manipulating, heart shatterer, should have listened to their momma. I was the devil she dreamed about.

Disobedient son, defiant, see no, hear no, commandments.

Gun toting, law breaker, on some gingerbread man shit.

Mine was theirs before the visit, shameless. Even shook the piggy bank. Thanked myself for every meal and slept past 3 on Sundays.

Always called home after the fact, cause I knew she would always love me.

These words are my mea culpa.

Mommy I am Truly Sorry.

ADAM'S CURSE

Deserted in an inkless world. Forbidden to create; asked not to dream. Blank pages; fragmented lead. Wingless birds; rhythm less music. Dull stars; colorless rainbows. Empty photos; fish that can't swim. An author without a story; a man without a soul.

DEAR JOHN

Inches away from home, moments away from death. Fluid rushes towards my lungs as I swallow all my tears. Speechless; unable to commit to verbal self retribution, physical victimization is outside of the realm of lines my temperament is willing to cross. I am reasonable; if he who owns the final gavel comes, I won't lie or beg.

Instead I will stand and admire his work.

I know my name is on the tongues of many, some I truly regret.

Others

Well, the removal of their sands was necessary. My need to survive outweighed the calling to be righteous...

Easy conclusion; Fish in a barrel

No second thought.

I didn't hide my intentions I repeatedly spoke on how I wanted more than what had been delivered to the door.

I warned that I would not starve, that if it was time to eat then hesitation would not cripple me.

My English is fluent, disbelief encouraged deafness.

Foolishness forced land dwellers to plunge into the deep end.

A shark only does what its natural instincts permit. The blame for its appetite is not his. I am not shamed for my love of conquest or craving to conquer.

The sorrow that drenches my soul is not due to my survival kit, just the uncertainty of walking a new path.

FENCE FULL OF HOLES

Nescient to the longevity of a pernicious vocabulary.
Assuming it would fade becoming as transparent as the
oxygen used to navigate these vessels of insults. Instead it
seems the characteristics resemble the eye worm.
Scar tissue covers the entry wound; the flesh heals quickly
but the damage is done.

Apology accepted; the brain accompanies the lips in
falsifying what the heart cannot.

Complete absolution is detained as anamnesis courses
through the victim's blood in an attempt to override the
thoughts of forgiveness.

Inconsideration can afflict beyond the tears we witness.

Beyond the outer walls; deep into the soul... all along the
fence

MY LETTER TO THE NEXT GEN

Hey Young World,

We are in desperate need for you to step up; grey heads are infusing your mind with Opioids; Methamphetamine, MDMA and LSD.

They have even legalized marijuana to ensure you have everything you need to lower your motivation. The belief that you can overcome these obstacles still burns in many of us. A new world is inescapable, this one has failed miserably.

Rapidly corroding as the powers that be dig tunnels for their dismount, like thieves in the night.

This is a now or never forecast; protect your investment or watch it fall like bad stock. Life is a game and a good team makes necessary adjustments at halftime. Understanding what did and didn't work in the first half.

Poor coaching and incompetent ownership; can forge a lackluster losing mentality.

Frightened by the notion of a system that no longer accepts their interpretation of "Just Us" and intimidated by equality. They have become desperate for your demise.

LET ME; BE ME

Trained to respect my elders and be polite.
I cuss a whole hell of a lot when I speak.
Let me; Be me
Told to walk with my head up and treat others how I want to be treated.
I would rather punch someone in the mouth than shake their hand.
Let me; Be me
Warned to fear God and follow in the path that Jesus made.
Stood on the corner and sold the drugs that man made.
Ask to do right by the opposite sex, not to play with their love or their mind.
I use them for sex and then step.
Let me; Be me
Raised to abide by the law and work for the things I wanted.
Bought a gun and a mask learn to take what I wanted.
Let me; Be me
Got older gained wisdom; had kids.
Understood I was foolish in my youth.
Thought about my family, decided to put some pride to my name.
Started walking a new path.
Let me; Be me
Bowed before the Father and The Son, begging for mercy.
Don't want to bring shame to my seeds.
Let me; Be me
Revised my thinking, reconstructed my lifestyle.

Ain't about the start, watch how I finish.
Let me; Be me

THE AWAKENING

Whispering to the wind relinquishing all my secrets; hoping that the stars don't hear my ugly truths.   Petrified... hands won't move, darkness reveals the light.

Wrong address... no halos at this house, should have listened a little closer.

Hard left at the fork, all signs said do right. Bull headed... blame it on the devil; seems to be the in thing, when your own thing doesn't work.

Wish there was a reset, bottle after bottle... emptied. No genie.

Opting for a plan Z; A through Y a story line of bad decisions and poor preparation.

Dead dream; dreamer, neck sore from looking back.

Scrap the game plan; no time for games, already placed a lot of calendars in the fire.

Proper English; dotting I's and crossing T's, dilute the street slang;

Elevating due to personal evaluation; lack of patience smashing down on the accelerator.

Prioritizing priorities; making life make sense.

Thought it through; deep thought everyday Pinky and The Brain.

Momma's baby learning to feed myself, so I can feed the rest.

Domino effects polish up the cap, clan full of kings and queens.

TALKING LIKE A JACKASS

The Word Hoarder is back, heard the growling of empty minds, time to restock the cupboard before the Cardinal dies.
Karen routed me here; this was never part of the plan. But, my peers keep jabbing at the stars yelling F THE MAN!
Corrupted politicians; politicking for the people on the paper, not the people in the paper.
Previously read the script; a rundown of artificial flavors and colors, used to call our intelligence into question.
Couldn't rig this election; popular vote got the job done.
Guess they see me like my lady, strong back, good tongue.
By any means necessary; the loaded weapon peeking out the curtains gaining ammo, courageous wordy wizard got the toupee in my cross hairs.
Too many smudges in the white house, so America played their Trump card.
First the wall then the chains, stoopid monkeys shoulda let the pistil late conduct; now liberal jackasses crying cause the elephants have the gun.
Donald Lynch; Grand Dragon, sheets and crosses on the lawn, annual messages full of subliminal plots to extract the melanin... Make It Great Again.
The plentiful few must have come on the wrong boat, missed all the greatness
Years of hell; less than a decade to change and believe, kneeling for the right to believe in a country that refuses to believe in us.

Way beyond the edge; free falling with no chute, like a bird with one wing, got "THE PEOPLE" at the door chanting Johnny we want our country back.

POMPOUS BEHAVIOUR

Overlook my decision to doze off, but I was unwilling to concentrate on the prelims, prefer to save the ink for championship rounds.
Judgmental hypocrites veering off in my lane, try to speak like the hoarder, not enough art in their brain.
Cerebrum malfunction too many shots to the head, déjà vu, running in circles, puppies chasing their tails.
Walk with me...
Wannabe cronies' stream to follow, then unfollow the game plan. Treacherous intentions obvious, continuously lining up offside, unwilling to coordinate.
Bush-league dancer; purposely stepping on toes.
Wordsmith golden gloves, stiff jab, busting their nose.
Cheating off my scripture; still failing miserably, the procedure too pristine.
Neanderthals; word mongering, banging your head against walls for a spark, when you're witnessing flame.
Growing with each keystroke, basking in the praises of those who understand the unusual.
Tooting my own horn...
Versatility God given, achieving on levels miles ahead of your heroes. I am what you dream to become.
The King of this workshop, ruler in this category, the true successor of this art gallery of words

MIND FUCKED

My thoughts have abandoned me in my moment of need without a moment.
Can I no longer feed those mentally starving for direction?
What has become of me? Brainwaves truncated and unresponsive.
Re-categorized: Pluto, fan base viewing me through a different lens.
Is this some sort of test; challenging me to expand my thoughts. Stepping further outside of the box of so-called normalcy.
Better yet is the intent to lure me back into a genre constructed solely on regularity?
In love with diversity; never seen the beauty in black and white.
Would rather chew razor blades and gargle battery acid than submit to common thought.
Open-mindedness supplies solace, deterring any notion of retracting my wings
Fearful of large crowds, allergic to sheep's wool, favor marching with the shepherd's hook.
The scent of wolves in the hills, flock losing faith, stars fade into darkness.
Word hoarder without the means to produce anything meaningful, the fabled hare in a tortoise race.
The unwilling victim of a MIND FUCK!

STILL NEEDS WORK

Redecorating the landscape by reconfiguring somber facial expressions
vastly improving the moral quality of all those willing to depart from their fortress of pride and reach for a hand.
A last ditch effort to gain a position alongside of those who believe in a life; after life, beyond the clouds.
Seeking to punch a ticket from acknowledgment for my newly found compassion for humankind. Rubber band man; stretching to accommodate, thinning out.
Refiling perspectives; alphabetical order, placing self behind others.
Uplifting the unfortunate by staying grounded, remembering the purpose of our existence.
Prior sins fuel me to be more angelic, striving not for perfection, merely for redemption.
Good Samaritan Dentistry; working on my DDS, one smile at a time.
Reminders that my brother still lurks, greed, jealous, impatient vocabulary... What about Me!!
Early riser, can't let that worm get away, still got a lot of work to do.

BROKEN PROMISE

Am I a ghost, unfit to rise to stubborn to fall? Where shall wandering tale me next?
I have been persuaded to become a leader on a journey to nowhere.
My mind jumps back and forth; looking for a place to rest, this pain is relentless, but I Fein for more of the same-
FEED ME
I am so hungry allow me to devour it all;
I am so deserving.
Whom better than me? Have not I proven that I am worthy, has not my rage shown you my value?
Can I not be granted the joys of all the tortured souls before me; why must I continue seen but not saw, touched but not felt?
What have I done to be left behind; must I bury more, tell me and I will provide you with what you seek.
Give me what is mine or I shall rip at their flesh, their eyes will witness my true form.
None will survive I will eat and eat until I am truly full, until you open your doors to me.
You promised that this world would suffer for my grief; why does it still laugh at me?

Facebook

https://www.facebook.com/mundy.mundy.144

Twitter

https://mobile.twitter.com/MundyMundy2018

Anchor

https://anchor.fm/mundy-mundy

https://www.breaker.audio/mundy-mundy

Email

thewordhoarder@gmail.com

www.ingramcontent.com/pod-product-compliance
Lightning Source LLC
Chambersburg PA
CBHW021444080526
44588CB00009B/687